CHINESE COOKING AT HOME

CHINESE COOKING AT HOME

Sumi Hatano

Broccoli with Prawns
西蘭花蝦球 (*Hsi-lan-hua-hsia-ch'iu*)
(*See page 86*)

DAVID & CHARLES
Newton Abbot   London

ISBN 0 7153 7873 2

First published in Japan by Shufunotomo Co Ltd,
1-chome, Surugadai, Kanda, Chiyoda-ku, Tokyo

First published in the United Kingdom by
David & Charles (Publishers) Ltd,
Newton Abbot, Devon, 1979

Foreword

I am indeed pleased to have my book on Chinese cooking published in English so that it can be shared with many people throughout the world.

You may wonder how a Japanese woman happened to become an authority on Chinese cooking. Let me tell you a little about the exciting experiences I had while living in Hong Kong from 1960 through 1965.

My husband, who works for one of the leading Japanese newspapers, the *Asahi Shimbun*, was transferred from Tokyo to Hong Kong and our whole family moved there for five years. It was there that my adventure in Chinese cooking started.

As you know, Hong Kong is known not only as a place for shopping, but also as a place for eating! There I found countless numbers of delicious Chinese foods gathered from all over China, and I was completely captivated by them. While my husband was busy visiting capitals and cities of neighboring countries, I took intensive courses in Chinese cooking. I attended schools and took private lessons with cooks, friends, and the servants who lived with us. In addition to these, we were indeed fortunate to have had many delightful associations with Chinese people who helped me understand more about Chinese cooking and its interesting background.

Ever since we returned to Tokyo, I have been actively engaged in teaching Chinese cooking through TV, newspapers and magazines, and so far I have published six books on the subject.

To me the essence of Chinese cuisine is its speed, simple cooking method and its delicious flavor. I hope you will find my recipes useful in your everyday cooking as well as for parties and that it will give you something new and exciting from the East !

Sumi Hatano

Sumi Hatano
Tokyo, Japan 1974

CONTENTS

● *All recipes are designed for four to six persons, unless otherwise stated.*
● *Wine in this book means Chinese wine, but dry sherry or sake (Japanese wine) can be used instead.*
● *Scallions are more familiarly known as Shallots.*
  Cornstarch is more familiarly known as flour.

Tableware for Chinese Dishes

Deep bowl (soup, dessert, etc.)

Large plate (assorted hors d'oeuvres, whole chicken, etc.)

Soup tureen

Individual bowl for rice and soup

Shakers for spices

Serving spoon

Individual soup spoon

Chopsticks

Medium-sized deep plate (stewed, braised, or steamed foods)

Platter (fish, chicken, etc.)

Individual medium-sized dinner dish

Individual small dish (for seasonings like soy sauce, mustard, etc.)

Medium-sized flat plate (sautéed and fried foods)

Kitchen Utensils

Please be flexible in using your own kitchen utensils when you cook Chinese-style. However, one thing I highly recommend is the *wok*, a round, all-purpose Chinese frying pan. Be sure to get one made of iron, not stainless steel. It is less expensive and cooks better.

Here are some typical utensils for Chinese cooking.

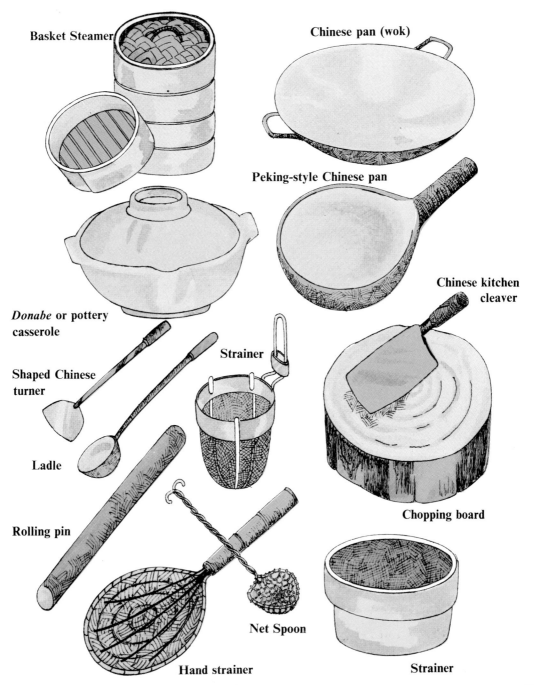

Basket Steamer

Chinese pan (wok)

Peking-style Chinese pan

Chinese kitchen cleaver

Donabe **or pottery casserole**

Shaped Chinese turner

Strainer

Ladle

Chopping board

Rolling pin

Net Spoon

Hand strainer

Strainer

How to Prepare Ingredients

Chinese cooking considers it important to cut ingredients in about the same size, not only for eye appeal but also for even cooking.

Here are some examples of cutting various ingredients in different shapes.

絲
Ssŭ: **Cut into strips or shred**

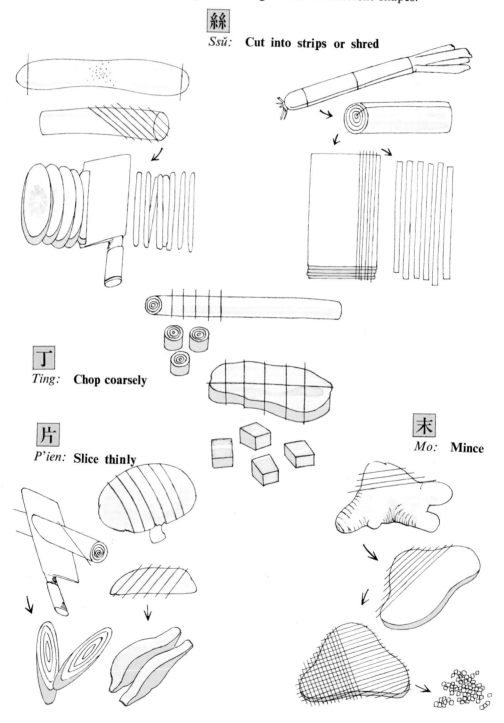

丁
Ting: **Chop coarsely**

片
P'ien: **Slice thinly**

末
Mo: **Mince**

條

T'iao: **Cut into sticks**

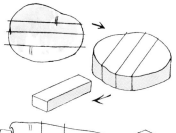

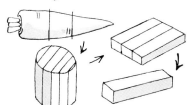

塊

K'uai: **Cube or dice**

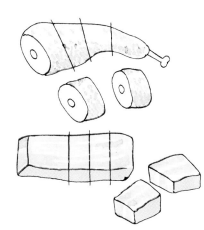

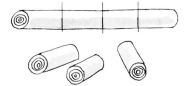

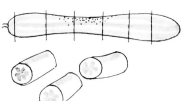

段

Tuan: **Cut into thick slices or chop into random lengths**

旋刀塊

Hsüan-tao-k'üai: **Cut into rolling cubes**

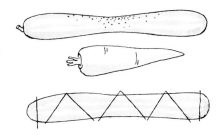

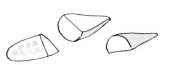

花

Hua: **Crisscross**

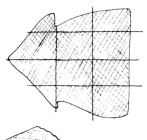

11

Cooking Techniques

*Stir Frying
炒 (ch'ao)

*Shallow Frying
煎 (chien)

*Deep-Frying
炸 (cha)

*Boiling, Stewing and Braising
煮 (chu)
煨 (wei)
燜 (mên)
滷 (lu)
燒 (shao)

*Steaming
蒸 (chêng)

*Baking or Grilling
烤 (kao)

*Double-Boiling
燉 (tun)

*Smoking
燻 (hsün)

*Mixing
涼拌 (liang-pan)

*Molding
凍 (tung)

*Dishes with thick sauce
溜 (liu)

BASIC METHODS

Deep-Fried Chicken

●炸　子　鶏(*Cha-tzu-chi*)*(See page 83)*

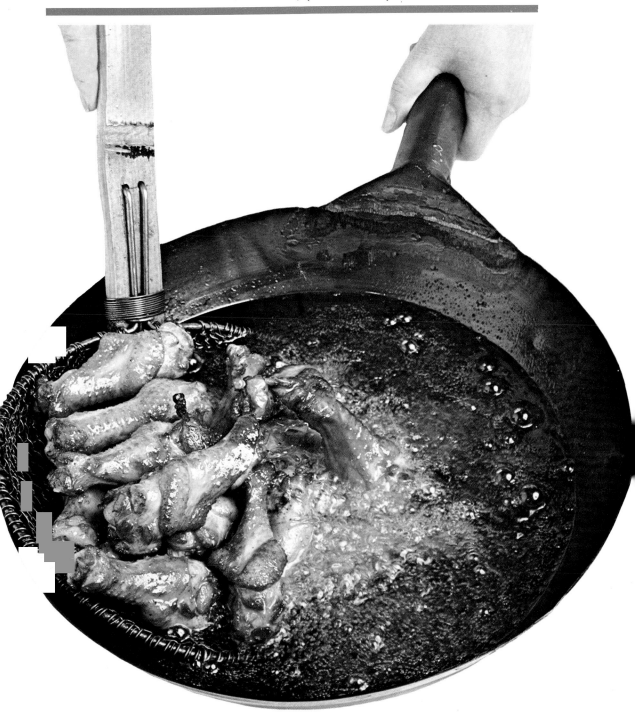

Sweet-Sour Fried Fish

● 西 湖 醋 魚 (*Hsi-hu-ts'u-yü*)

Ingredients:

1¼ lb. flatfish, cleaned, washed, drained and crisscross slashes
   made on black side   **(1)**
1 teaspoon minced garlic
1 dried hot red pepper, seeded and cut in round slices
1 oz. carrots, finely shredded, soaked in Mixture B for 30 minutes
1 oz. pickled slices of ginger
1 oz. pickled small onions
⅓ green onion (white part), finely shredded, soaked in water and drained
cooking oil
sesame oil
cornstarch for coating fish
1 tablespoon cornstarch, dissolved in 2 tablespoons water

Mixture A
- 1 teaspoon soy sauce
- 1 teaspoon sesame oil
- dash of pepper

Mixture B
- 3 tablespoons sugar
- 3 tablespoons vinegar
- ½ teaspoon salt

Mixture C
- ⅔ cup vinegar
- ⅔ cup sugar
- 3 tablespoons tomato catsup
- 2½ tablespoons Worcestershire sauce
- 2½ teaspoons salt

Instructions:

1. Sprinkle Mixture A on both sides of fish, then coat thoroughly with cornstarch, using sifter. Deep-fry over medium heat. Drain well and set aside. **(2–3)**

2. Heat 2 tablespoons cooking oil in pan and sauté garlic, hot red pepper, carrots, pickled ginger and onions. Add Mixture C and bring to boil. Thicken with dissolved cornstarch. Just before removing from heat, sprinkle with a few drops of sesame oil for flavor. **(4)**

3. Place fried fish on platter. Pour the sauce over it. Garnish with shredded green onion. **(5)**

Spring Rolls

● 春　捲 (*Ch'un-chuan*)

Ingredients:

10 sheets spring roll wrappings(see page 90)
$\frac{1}{2}$ lb. lean pork, thinly sliced and shredded
$\frac{1}{3}$ lb. small shrimp, shelled, cleaned and drained
$\frac{1}{2}$ lb. bean sprouts, washed and drained
4 dried Chinese mushrooms, soaked, stems removed, squeezed and shredded
1 egg, pan-fried flat in a thin omelet and cut into julienne strips
3–5 scallions, cut into 2-inch lengths

2 teaspoons cornstarch, dissolved in 4 teaspoons water
cooking oil
flour mixed with enough water to form thick paste

Mixture A
- 2 tablespoons soup stock
- 1 tablespoon oyster sauce
- 1 tablespoon soy sauce
- 1 teaspoon sugar
- 1 teaspoon salt
- dash of sesame oil and pepper

Instructions:

1. Sauté bean sprouts and scallions quickly in 1 tablespoon hot oil. Remove from heat, drain, and set aside. **(2)**
2. Heat 2 tablespoons cooking oil in pan; mix in and sauté quickly pork, shrimp, mushrooms, and egg strips. Then add cooked bean sprouts and scallions. Add Mixture A, stirring constantly, and thicken with dissolved cornstarch. **(3–4)**
3. Place one tenth of the filling on the lower half of each wrapping. Roll up and seal lightly by brushing edges with flour paste. **(6–7)**
4. Fry in deep oil until crisp and golden brown. **(8)**

5

6

7

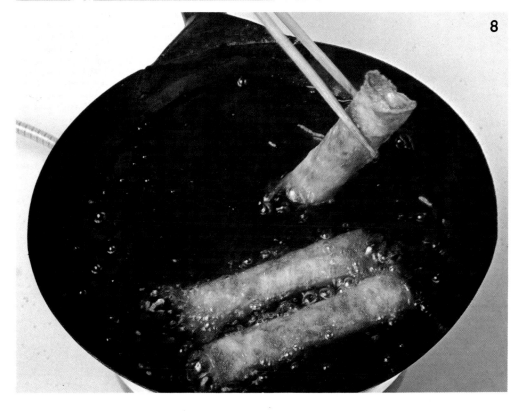

8

Fried Spicy Prawns

● 干燒明蝦 (*Kan-shao-ming-hsia*)

Ingredients:
 1 lb. prawns
 1 green onion or scallion, minced
 1-inch piece fresh ginger, minced
 1 tablespoon wine
 cooking oil

Mixture A
 1 tablespoon *tou-pan-chiang* (Brown Bean Sauce) or 2 teaspoons Tabasco
 1 tablespoon tomato catsup
 1 teaspoon soy sauce
 $\frac{1}{3}$ teaspoon salt

Instructions:
 1. Wash prawns, remove tail tips and black veins, cut into two or three pieces, and wipe off thoroughly. Squeeze out water from each tail tip. **(1–4)**
 2. Fry prawns in deep oil. As soon as color turns red, remove from pan and set aside. **(5)**
 3. Sauté minced green onion and ginger in 3 tablespoons hot oil. Add prawns and sauté quickly and thoroughly. Sprinkle with wine and add Mixture A, stirring quickly over high heat until done. **(6–7)**

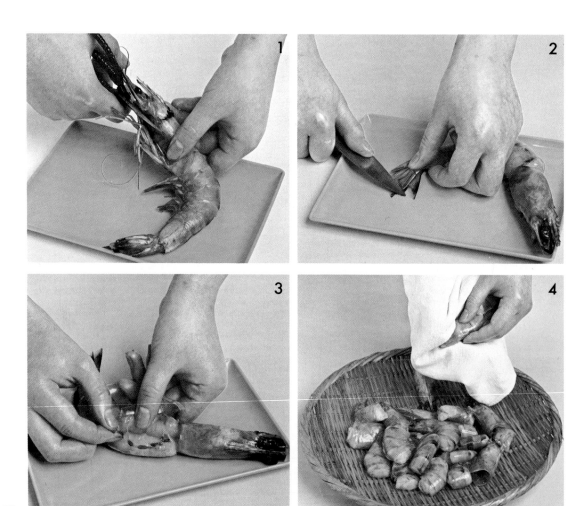

5

6

7

19

Shredded Beef with Bamboo Shoots and Green Peppers

● 魚香牛肉 (*Yü-hsiang-niu-jou*)

Ingredients:

½ lb. beef, shredded
½ egg white
1 teaspoon cornstarch
¼ teaspoon salt
5 green peppers, shredded
4 oz. boiled bamboo shoots, shredded
1 clove garlic, minced
1-inch piece fresh ginger, minced

½ green onion or scallion, minced
1 tablespoon wine
dash of sesame oil
cooking oil

Mixture A
{
2½ tablespoons soy sauce
1 teaspoon sugar
1 teaspoon vinegar
}

Instructions:

1. Dip shredded beef in egg white mixed with cornstarch and salt. Fry slowly in deep oil over low heat until color turns pale. **(1)**

2. In 3 tablespoons hot oil, sauté garlic, ginger and green onion. Add first green peppers, then bamboo shoots, and finally beef. **(2–5)**

3. Sprinkle with wine, stir in Mixture A, and cook quickly over high heat. Just before removing from heat, sprinkle with sesame oil for flavor. **(6)**

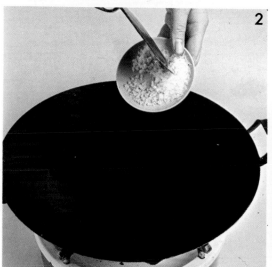

Cubed Pork with Nuts, Szechwan Style

● 宮保肉丁 (*Kung-pao-jou-ting*)

Ingredients:

1½ oz. peanuts
11 oz. lean pork, cut into ½-inch cubes

Mixture A
- ½ egg white
- 1 teaspoon cornstarch
- dash of salt

1–2 dried hot red peppers, seeded and cut into round slices
2 cloves garlic, minced
4 green onions (white part), chopped into ½-inch pieces
2 fresh green peppers (long-shaped and small in size), cut into ½-inch squares
1 tablespoon wine
1 teaspoon cornstarch dissolved in 2 teaspoons water
cooking oil
dash of monosodium glutamate

Mixture B
- 1 tablespoon dark soybean paste
- 1 tablespoon soy sauce
- 2 teaspoons sugar
- ½ teaspoon vinegar
- ¼ teaspoon salt

Instructions:

1. Fry peanuts in deep oil over medium heat until light brown. Quickly remove from pan. **(1)**
2. Put cubed pork in bowl and coat with Mixture A. **(2)**
   Deep-fry slowly over low heat just until meat turns pale. Remove from pan and set aside.
3. In 3 tablespoons hot oil, sauté garlic and red pepper first, then green onion and green pepper. Add fried pork and sprinkle with wine. Stir in Mixture B and sauté quickly and thoroughly, adding dash of monosodium glutamate. Thicken with dissolved cornstarch. Just before removing from heat, quickly mix in fried peanuts and stir well to finish. **(3–5)**

Note:

Walnuts may also be used. Soak in warm water until swollen. Peel carefully and wipe off before frying. **(A, B)**

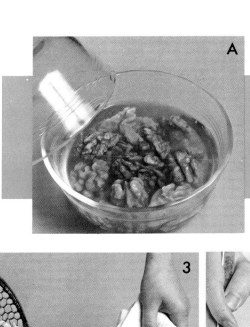

A

B

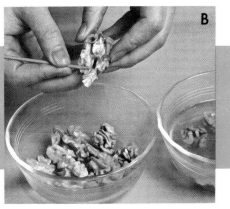

5

3

4

Stewed Pork and Crab Meat Balls

● 蟹 粉 獅 子 頭 (*Hsieh-fên-shih-tzu-tou*)

Ingredients:

14 oz. ground lean pork, lightly pounded
with sharp edge of knife **(1)**

1 can (4 oz.) crab meat, boned, flaked and
drained

1 green onion or scallion, quartered lengthwise, then cut into $\frac{1}{4}$-inch sticks

1 tablespoon juice from grated fresh ginger

$\frac{1}{2}$ teaspoon salt

1 tablespoon cornstarch

$\frac{1}{2}$ Chinese cabbage, core removed, cut

lengthwise in half, then cut into 2-inch
widths

$\frac{1}{4}$ cup water, flavored with small amounts of
thinly sliced fresh ginger and finely shredded green onion

3 cups soup stock

cooking oil

1 tablespoon wine

2 tablespoons soy sauce

2 teaspoons sugar

Instructions:

1. Combine ground pork, crab meat, and green onion in bowl. Add ginger juice, salt, and cornstarch and mix well by hand. Gradually add flavored water, mixing thoroughly. Divide the mixture in 4 portions and make large meat balls. Deep-fry carefully over medium heat until light brown. **(2–5)**

2. Sauté quickly sliced Chinese cabbage in 3 tablespoons hot oil. Remove to pottery casserole or deep heavy saucepan. **(6)**

3. Place meat balls on Chinese cabbage and sprinkle with wine. Add soup stock and season with sugar and soy sauce. Cover and cook first 15 minutes over high heat. Reduce heat and simmer over low heat about 45 minutes. Serve hot with spoon. **(7)**

5

6

7

Stewed Spiced Pork

● 東　坡　肉(*Tung-po-jou*)

Ingredients:

- 1½ lb. pork (block of fresh bacon)
- 2 green onions or scallions, cut into 4-inch lengths and tied together
- 3 tablespoons wine
- ½ cup soy sauce
- 2 tablespoons sugar
- 1 bunch spinach, washed and cleaned
- 3 tablespoons cooking oil
- 1 teaspoon salt
- 1 cup water

Spices:

Names of spices in the photo are: from left on top, *kan-t'sao*, fennel seeds, *san-jou*, *yuan-sui-mi*, *ta-hui*, cinnamon sticks, *t'sao-kuo* and *hua-chiao*. Place small amounts of these spices in a cheesecloth bag, and tie firmly.

Instructions:

1. Place pork in boiling water. Bring back to boiling and remove. **(1)**
2. Place dried bamboo skin on bottom of pottery or heavy pan to avoid scorching, and place pork on it, fat side down. Add tied-up green onions and spice bag, then wine, soy sauce, and sugar. Pour in just enough hot water to cover the meat. Cover and cook over medium heat 30 minutes. Reduce heat and gently simmer 1½ hours. **(2–6)**
3. Sauté spinach in pan and season with salt. Add a little more salt and water and cover for steaming effect. **(7)**

   Cut cooked meat into ½-inch slices and arrange on cooked spinach.

n-t 'sao

nel seeds

san-jou

n-sui-mi

ta-hui

cinnamon sticks   ts'ao-kuo   hua-chiao

5

6

7

27

Braised Chicken Liver

● 紅焼鶏肝 (*Hung-shao-chi-kan*)

Ingredients:

14 oz. chicken livers, thoroughly washed and cut into halves   **(A-D)**
½ green onion or scallion, cut into 2-inch lengths
1-inch piece fresh ginger, thinly sliced and lightly
    pounded with dull edge of knife

Mixture A
- 4 tablespoons soy sauce
- 1 tablespoon sugar
- 1 tablespoon wine
- 2 cups water
- dash of monosodium glutamate

1 star anise

Instructions:

1. Place liver in boiling water. Bring back to boiling and drain.   **(1)**
2. Put in heavy kettle and add Mixture A, star anise, green onion and ginger. Braise over medium heat until almost no liquid is left in kettle.   **(2–4)**

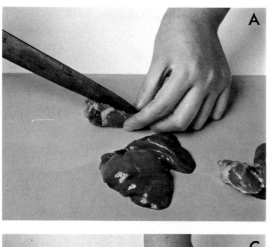
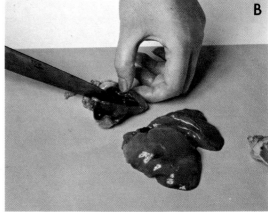
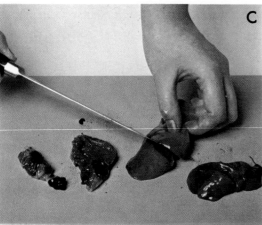
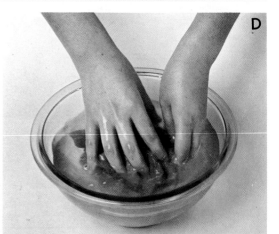

Sweet-Sour Pork

● 咕 咾 肉 (*Ku-lao-jou*)

Ingredients:

$\frac{3}{4}$ pound lean pork, cut into 1-inch bite-size pieces and lightly pounded **(1)**
1 egg, lightly beaten
cornstarch for coating
2 green onions, cut into 1-inch lengths
2 green peppers, seeded, cut into bite-size pieces
4 slices pineapple, drained and cut into bite-size pieces
1 clove garlic, minced
1 dried hot red pepper, seeded, cut in round slices
1 tablespoon wine
2 teaspoons cornstarch, dissolved in 4 teaspoons water
oil

Sweet-Sour Sauce: (Mix well together beforehand.)
    $\frac{1}{3}$ cup vinegar
    1 tablespoon soy sauce
    $4\frac{1}{2}$ tablespoons sugar
    1 tablespoon tomato catsup
    2 tablespoons Worcestershire sauce
    $\frac{1}{2}$ teaspoon salt

Instructions:

1. With fingers dip the pieces of pork in the beaten egg and roll them over cornstarch for frying. **(2)**
2. Fry in oil over medium heat until light brown. Drain. **(3)**
3. Quickly sauté garlic in 3 tablespoons oil; then add red pepper, green pepper, green onion, pineapple, and pork. Stir well. Sprinkle with wine, stir in the sweet-sour sauce, and bring to boil. While boiling, add dissolved cornstarch and stir well until the mixture is thick and clear. Remove from heat and serve warm. **(4–7)**

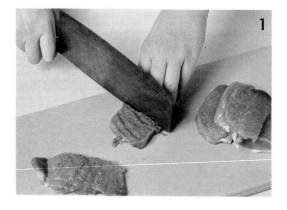

Fried Egg with Crab Meat

● 芙 蓉 蟹(*Fu-jung-hsieh*)

Ingredients:

1 can (7 oz.) crab meat, boned, flaked, drained and sprinkled with 1 tablespoon wine

6 eggs

2 or 3 dried Chinese mushrooms, soaked, stems removed, and shredded

4 oz. boiled bamboo shoots, shredded

$\frac{1}{4}$ cup peas

$\frac{1}{2}$ teaspoon salt

1 teaspoon cornstarch, dissolved in 2 teaspoons water

cooking oil

Mixture A
- 1$\frac{1}{2}$ cup soup stock
- 1 tablespoon soy sauce
- 1 teaspoon sugar
- dash of monosodium glutamate

Instructions:

1. Beat eggs lightly. Add crab meat and salt. **(1)**
2. Heat pan (Chinese style preferred) and pour in 3 tablespoons cooking oil. Continue heating until bottom and sides of pan are thoroughly greased and hot. Gently pour egg-crab mixture into pan over high heat. When center part is half set, turn over and fry other side. Remove to plate. **(2–3)**
3. Sauté prepared mushrooms, bamboo shoots and peas in 2 tablespoons hot oil. Add Mixture A, stirring constantly. Thicken with dissolved cornstarch and pour over the fried egg-crab mixture. **(4)**

Fried Egg, Shanghai Style

芙蓉炒蟹粉
(*Fu-jung-ch'ao-hsieh-fên*)

(*Continued on page 84*)

Fried Egg with Crab Meat

33

Noodles with Chinese Meat Sauce

● 炸 醬 麵 (*Cha-chiang-mien*)

Ingredients:

Desired kind of noodles for 4 persons, boiled, drained, and sprinkled with sesame oil to prevent sticking together **(A, B)**
3 lb. ground pork
3 dried Chinese mushrooms, soaked, stems removed, and shredded
1 cucumber, shredded
4 cups bean sprouts, boiled, sprinkled with little vinegar, and drained **(C)**

1 clove garlic, minced
1 cup soup stock
4 tablespoons soy sauce
2½ tablespoons sugar
4 tablespoons dark soybean paste
1 tablespoon cornstarch, dissolved in 2 tablespoons water
sesame oil
cooking oil

Instructions:

1. Sauté garlic first in 3 tablespoons hot oil and add ground pork and mushrooms, stirring well. Gradually add soup stock, soy sauce, sugar and soybean paste and bring to boil. **(1–2)**
2. Thicken with dissolved cornstarch, and pour over warm (or cold) noodles. Garnish with cucumber and bean sprouts.

Sour Pepper Fish Soup

●黄　魚　湯 (*Huang-yü-t'ang*)

Ingredients:
   3 fillets of white meat fish
   ¼ green onion or scallion, minced
   1-inch piece fresh ginger, minced
   1 tablespoon wine
   6 cups soup stock
   2 tablespoons soy sauce
   3 tablespoons vinegar
   1 teaspoon white pepper
   3 tablespoons cornstarch, dissolved in 6 tablespoons water
   2 eggs, lightly beaten

Instructions:
   1. Place fish in bowl and sprinkle with green onion, ginger, and wine. Steam 10 minutes over medium heat. Remove bones and skin, if any, and coarsely flake fish.   **(1–3)**
   2. Combine fish and soup stock in pan. Season with soy sauce, vinegar, and white pepper and bring to boil. Thicken with dissolved cornstarch. Bring to boil again and pour beaten eggs slowly into soup.   **(4–6)**
   3. When eggs are half set, stir well and serve hot.

Steamed Chicken

●白　切　鶏(*Pai-ch'ieh-chi*)

Ingredients:
- 1 whole chicken (about 2 lb.)
- ½ green onion cut in 2-inch lengths lightly strack with the flat of knife to release flavor
- 1-inch fresh ginger, thinly sliced and struck with the blunt flat to release flavor **(1)**
- ¼ cup wine
- 1 teaspoon salt

Instructions:
1. Wash chicken and wipe off thoroughly. Rub in salt. Put green onion and ginger into stomach cavity. Place chicken on dish and sprinkle with wine. **(2–4)**
2. Steam chicken over high heat for about 20 minutes. (Cooking time varies a little according to the size of the chicken.) Cool. **(5)**
3. Cut off thigh on both sides, then split breast in half and cut off wings. **(A–B)**
   Slice meat, bones and all, into about ½-inch wide pieces. Arrange on platter and serve with seasonings like soy sauce, vinegar, hot sauce and mustard.

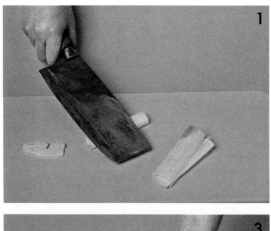

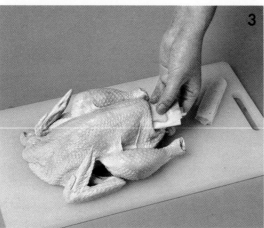

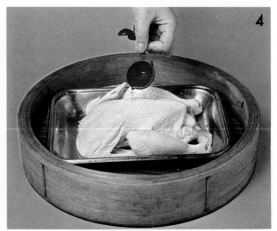

5

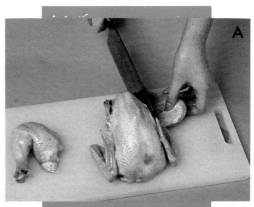

A

B

Fried Rice

● 揚州炒飯 (*Yang-chou-ch'ao-fan*)

Ingredients:
  3 cups rice
  3–4 dried Chinese mushrooms
  2 eggs, lightly beaten
  6 oz. small shrimps, shelled
  6 oz. boneless chicken, cut into $\frac{1}{2}$-inch cubes
  1 egg white
  2 teaspoons cornstarch
  6 oz. roasted pork, cut into $\frac{1}{2}$-inch cubes
  $\frac{1}{2}$ cup peas, boiled
  $\frac{1}{2}$ cup soup stock
  dash of soy sauce, salt, sugar, wine, sesame oil, pepper, and monosodium glutamate
  cooking oil

Instructions:
  1. Wash rice and drain for an hour before cooking in $3\frac{1}{2}$ cups water. After removing from heat, let stand covered at least 10 minutes.
  2. Soak Chinese mushrooms in 1 cup water until tender. Remove stems. To the mushroom water add dash of soy sauce, salt, sugar, sesame oil and monosodium glutamate. Return mushrooms to the seasoned water and steam 15 minutes. Cut into $\frac{1}{2}$-inch squares.
  3. Using fingers, thoroughly coat chicken and shrimp with a mixture of egg white and cornstarch. Fry slowly over low heat just until colors change. Drain and set aside. **(1)**
  4. Add dash of salt to lightly beaten eggs and fry quickly in 2 teaspoons hot oil, stirring constantly to scramble. **(2)**
  5. Heat 4–5 tablespoons cooking oil in big pan (Chinese style preferred), add mushrooms, shrimps, chicken and roasted pork. Sprinkle with 1 tablespoon wine and 1 teaspoon salt and quickly sauté over medium heat. **(3)**
  6. Mix in cooked rice and again sprinkle with 1 teaspoon salt, dash of pepper and monosodium glutamate. Add boiled peas and scrambled eggs, mixing thoroughly and quickly over high heat. Add soup stock. Serve warm. **(4–7)**

Steam-Baked Meat Pies

● 鍋 貼 餃 子 (*Kuo-t'ieh-chiao-tzu*)

Ingredients:

9 oz. ground pork, lightly pounded with sharp edge of knife
3½ tablespoons soy sauce
1½ tablespoons sesame oil
dash of monosodium glutamate
10 oz. Chinese cabbage leaves, boiled, completely drained by hand-wringing, and minced
2–3 dried Chinese mushrooms, soaked, stems removed, and minced
3½ oz. boiled bamboo shoots, minced
½ green onion or scallion, minced
1-inch fresh ginger, minced
35–40 small pastry rounds (bought ready-made, or see recipe on page 88)
vinegar, mustard, soy sauce and *tou-pan-chiang* (brown bean sauce)

Instructions:

1. Thoroughly mix ground pork, soy sauce, sesame oil, monosodium glutamate, Chinese cabbage, mushrooms, bamboo shoots, green onion, and ginger to make the filling.
2. Place about 1½ teaspoons of filling in center of each pie shell. Bring opposite edges together, making pleats on one edge. Seal well by dotting with water, if necessary, and make into crescent shapes. **(1–3)**
3. Heat small amount of cooking oil in skillet and place pies, pleated side up, in two lines. Cook over high heat, quickly browning bottom side. Pour hot water into skillet to a depth of about ½-inch. Cover, reduce heat, and steam-bake until no liquid is left in skillet. **(4–5)**
4. Remove cover. Cover skillet again with plate turned upside down. Turn skillet over on plate to have browned side up for serving. **(6–7)**
5. Serve warm with soy sauce, mustard, vinegar, and hot sauce.

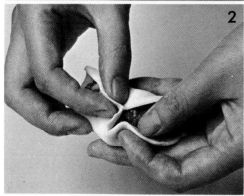

Soft Chinese Meat Cakes

● 叉 燒 包(*Ch'a-shao-pao*)

Ingredients:

For Dough:
11 oz. flour
1 tablespoon baking powder
4 oz. sugar
2 tablespoons lard
1 teaspoon vinegar
1 cup water

For Filling:
3 oz. roast pork, thinly sliced and cut into pieces
$\frac{1}{2}$ green onion or scallion, minced

1 clove garlic, minced

Sauce
$\frac{1}{2}$ cup soup stock
1 tablespoon sugar
1 tablespoon soy sauce
1 tablespoon oyster sauce
dash of pepper
few drops of sesame oil

cooking oil
2 tablespoons cornstarch, dissolved in 4 tablespoons water
wax paper

Instructions:

1. Sift together flour and baking powder. Add sugar, lard, vinegar and water and mix thoroughly with hand until soft. Place damp cloth over the dough and let stand 10 minutes. **(1)**

2. Sauté minced green onion and garlic in 3 tablespoons hot oil. Mix in the sauce and bring to boil. Add pork pieces and dissolved cornstarch to thicken. Let cool. **(A, B)**

3. Place dough on board dusted with flour and shape into a thick roll. Using knife, cut into 12 portions. Place cut side up on board and press surface with hand to make round wrapping about 3 inches in diameter. **(2–3)**

4. When meat filling is cool, put 1 tablespoon in center of each wrapping; wrap and seal carefully making some pleats in center. **(4)**

5. Place each cake on a small piece of wax paper to prevent sticking to steamer. Steam quickly over high heat for 10 minutes. Remove to plate and serve warm. **(5)**

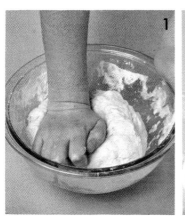

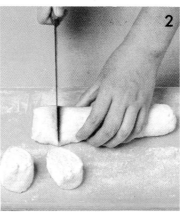

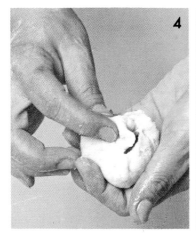

Almond Jelly

● 杏仁豆腐 (*Hsing-jên-tou-fu*)

Ingredients:

1 stick *kanten*, washed, lightly squeezed and torn into coarse pieces (or 2 envelopes unflavored gelatin*)

3 cups water

1 cup sugar

$\frac{1}{2}$ cup evaporated milk

$\frac{1}{2}$ teaspoon almond extract

1 can fruit cocktail (with syrup) or other desired kind of canned fruits

Instructions:

1. Boil water and add *kanten* pieces until completely dissolved. Stir in sugar, and remove from heat. Pour into flat container using strainer. **(1–3)**

2. Add evaporated milk stirring constantly. When slightly cooled, mix in almond extract and set aside until cold. Chill in refrigerator. **(4)**

3. Cut into diamond shapes and remove to serving dish. **(5)**
   Pour syrup from canned fruit over the diamonds and garnish with the fruit.

* *When using gelatin instead of* kanten, *add 2 tablespoons cold water to 2 tablespoons unflavored gelatin and stir to soften, then add 1 cup boiling water to dissolve completely.*

Tossed Bean Threads with Bean Sprouts

● 涼拌粉絲豆芽 (*Liang-pan-fên-ssǔ-tou-ya*)

Ingredients:

- 1 oz. dry bean threads
- 5 cups bean sprouts, washed and drained
- ⅓ stalk green onion, thinly bias-cut

Mixture A
- 4 tablespoons vinegar
- 2 teaspoons salt
- 2 teaspoons sesame oil
- dash of monosodium glutamate

Instructions:

1. Pour Mixture A into a bowl. Add prepared green onion and stir well. **(1)**
2. Soak bean threads in hot water until soft and transparent. Cut into 4-inch lengths. Drain well. **(2–3)**
3. Boil bean sprouts quickly (being careful not to overcook) and drain. **(4)**
4. While bean sprouts are hot, toss quickly in (1). Then, add drained bean threads and mix well. Refrigerate and serve cold. **(5)**

Typical Menu

Continued on pages 62–64

**Tossed Cucumber with Hot Bean Paste
Braised Chicken Gizzards
Sweet-Sour Pork
Corn Chicken Soup**

Simple Recipes

Continued on pages 65–67

Fried Scallops, Sautéed Eggplants, Crab Meat with Mushrooms, Chinese Sautéed Pork and Tossed Bean Threads with Bean Sprouts

Quick and Easy Recipes

Continued on pages 68–72

Tossed Bean Curd,
Sautéed Ground Meat
with Peas,
Creamy Chinese
Cabbage,
Chicken with Lemon
Sauce and
Curried Shrimp

Recipes for Gourmets

Continued on pages 73–77

Spinach and Egg Soup,
Lemon Flavored Chicken,
Chow-mein and
Beef Steak, Chinese Style

Hors d'Oeuvres

Continued on pages 78–82

Hors d'Oeuvres
(Sweet-Sour Chinese Cabbage, Sautéed Chinese Mushrooms,
Savory Prawns, Steamed Chicken, Molded *P'i-tan* Eggs,
Vinegared Jelly fish with Cucumber),
Fried Honey Walnuts and Tossed Celery, Shanghai Style

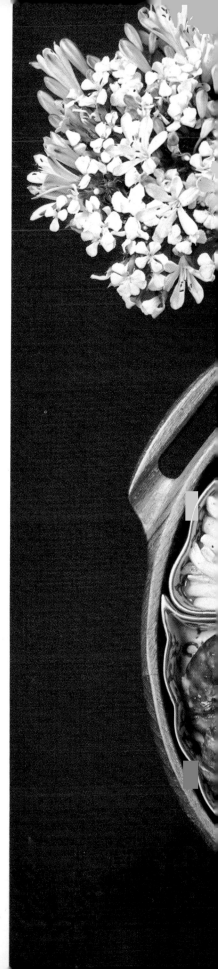

58

Chinese Vegetables

1 Chinese Cabbage, White
2 Snow Peas
3 Giant White Radish
4 Bean Sprouts
5 Celery Cabbage
6 Lima Beans
7 Chinese Parsley
8 Water Chestnuts
9 Chinese Mushrooms,
10 Ginger Roots
11 Bamboo Shoot

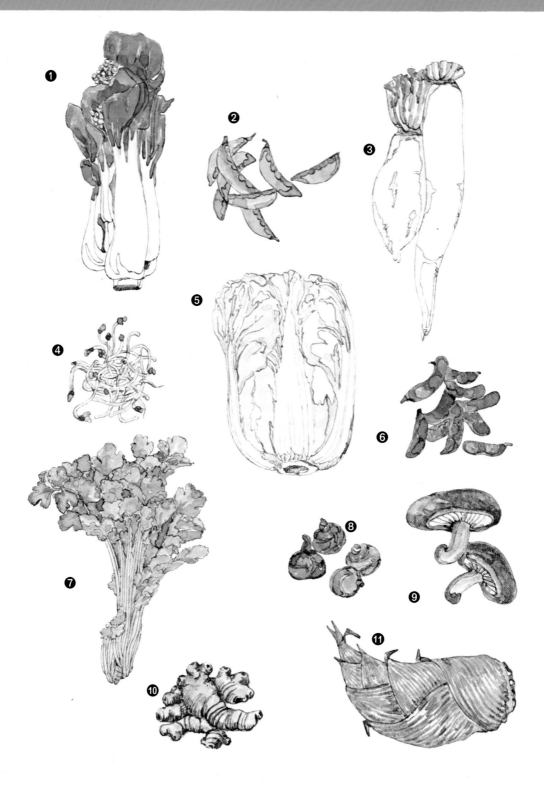

Typical Menu

Continued from page 50

Tossed Cucumber with Hot Bean Paste
麻辣黃瓜
(*Ma-la-huang-kua*)

Braised Chicken Gizzards
滷 鷄 腎
(*Lu-chi-shên*)

Sweet-Sour Pork
咕 咾 肉
(*Ku-lao-jou*)

Corn Chicken Soup
鷄茸粟米
(*Chi-jung-su-mi*)

Tossed Cucumber with Hot Bean Paste

麻辣黃瓜
(*Ma-la-huang-kua*)

Ingredients:

4 medium cucumbers, washed
1 teaspoon salt

Mixture A
- 1 tablespoon *tou-pan-chiang* (or 1 hot red pepper, seeded and minced)
- 1 teaspoon soy sauce
- 1 teaspoon seasame oil
- dash of monosodium glutamate

Instructions:

1 Cut cucumbers coarsely in cubes and sprinkle with salt. Let stand until slightly soft, then wash and wipe off lightly.

2. Pour Mixture A over the cucumber and marinate in refrigerator for 20 to 30 minutes. Serve cold in deep dish.

62

Braised Chicken Gizzards

滷 鷄 腎
(*Lu-chi-shên*)

Ingredients:
   10 whole chicken gizzards
   1 green onion, cut in 2-inch lengths
   1 slice fresh ginger, peeled and crushed
   1 parsley for garnish

Mixture A
   4 tablespoons soy sauce
   1 tablespoon sugar
   2 tablespoons wine
   1 cup water

Instructions:
   1. Place gizzards in cold water to cover, and bring to a boil. Remove fat, wash well and drain.
   2. In a heavy skillet bring Mixture A to boil. Add gizzards, green onion, and ginger. Cover and simmer for about 30 minutes until very little sauce is left in skillet.
   3. Cool, then slice lengthwise and arrange on serving dish. Garnish with parsley, if desired.

Sweet–Sour Pork

咕 咾 肉 (*Ku-lao-jou*)

See page 30

Corn Chicken Soup

鶏茸粟米
(*Chi-jung-su-mi*)

Ingredients:

$\frac{1}{2}$ 1b. ground chicken breast
2 egg whites, stiffly beaten
1 can sweet corn (cream style)
2 cups chicken stock
$\frac{1}{2}$ teaspoon salt
1 tablespoon cornstarch, dissolved in 2 tablespoons water
small amount of minced parsley

Instructions:

1. Gradually bring the chicken stock to boil and add the corn. Just before it gets to boiling point, stir in the ground chicken with a wire whisk and add salt. While boiling, stir in dissolved cornstarch until it thickens.

2. Remove from heat and quickly fold in the beaten egg whites.

3. Garnish with minced parsley and serve immediately.

Simple Recipes

Continued from page 52

Chinese Sautéed Pork
京 都 排 骨 (*Ching-tu-p'ai-ku*)

Crabmeat with Mushrooms
蟹 扒 鮮 菇 (*Hsieh-pa-hsien-ku*)

Fried Scallops
生 燒 帶 子 (*Sheng-shao-tai-tzu*)

Sautéed Eggplants
干 燒 茹 子 (*Kan-shao-ch'ieh-tzu*)

Tossed Bean Threads with Bean Sprouts
涼拌粉絲豆芽 (*Liang-pan-fên-ssu-tou-ya*)

Chinese Sautéed Pork

京 都 排 骨
(*Ching-tu-p'ai-ku*)

Ingredients:
- 1 lb. lean pork, cut into 2 × 3-inch pieces and pounded lightly with the blunt edge of knife
- 1 egg, lightly beaten
- cornstarch
- 2 green onions, cut into 1-inch lengths
- 1 clove garlic, minced
- 1 dried hot red pepper, seeded and cut in round slices
- 1 tablespoon wine
- cooking oil

Mixture A
- 2 tablespoons soy sauce
- 2 tablespoons sugar
- 1 tablespoon soy bean paste
- 1 tablespoon Worcestershire sauce

Instructions:
1. Dip pork into beaten egg, dredge with cornstarch, and fry in deep oil. Drain.
2. Sauté garlic and green onions in 3 tablespoons hot oil, stirring well.
3. Stir in fried pork and red pepper. Heat, then sprinkle with wine. Add Mixture A and cook over high heat till pork is done.

Crab Meat with Mushrooms

蟹 扒 鮮 菇
(*Hsieh-pa-hsien-ku*)

Ingredients:

1 small can sliced mushrooms, drained
1 7-oz. can crab meat, flaked in large pieces
1 tablespoon wine
Mixture A $\begin{cases} \frac{1}{3} \text{ cup soup stock} \\ \frac{1}{4} \text{ teaspoon salt} \end{cases}$
dash of monosodium glutamate, sesame oil, and pepper
1 teaspoon cornstarch, dissolved in 2 teaspoons water
cooking oil

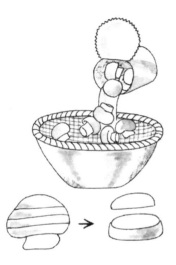

Instructions:

1. Sauté crab meat and mushrooms in 2 tablespoons hot oil and sprinkle with wine. Add Mixture A. Stir in dissolved cornstarch to thicken the mixture.

2. Sprinkle with sesame oil for glaze and pepper to taste. Remove to plate and serve warm.

* *If fresh mushrooms are preferred, they should be washed and cut in halves. Then boil, immerse in water, and drain well before cooking.*

Fried Scallops

生 燒 帶 子
(*Shêng-shao-tai-tzu*)

Ingredients:

14 oz. scallops, washed, skinned, and sliced into $\frac{1}{3}$-inch pieces
1 egg, beaten
cornstarch
cooking oil

Mixture A {
1 tablespoon light-colored soy sauce
1 tablespoon wine
1 tablespoon juice from grated and squeezed fresh ginger
1 teaspoon sugar
½ teaspoon salt
few drops of sesame or salad oil
dash of monosodium glutamate
}

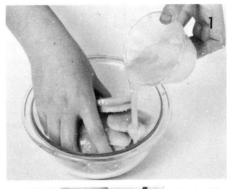

Instructions:
1. Soak prepared scallops in Mixture A for 10 minutes. Drain well. **(1)**
2. Dip into beaten egg and roll in cornstarch. Quickly fry over medium heat until light brown. Serve while warm. **(2)**

Sautéed Eggplant

干焼茄子
(*Kan-shao-ch'ieh-tzu*)

Ingredients:
6 eggplants (Amer. ones are big.) Mediumsized one is above 1½ lb.
½ green onion, minced
1 clove garlic, minced
1 slice fresh ginger, minced
cooking oil

Mixture A {
1 tablespoon soy sauce
1 tablespoon sugar
½ teaspoon salt
dash of monosodium glutamate
}

Instructions:
1. Cut eggplant crosswise into rounds 3 or 4 inches thick, then cut the rounds lengthwise into 2-inch thick sticks.
2. Fry quickly in deep oil and set aside.
3. Sauté minced green onion, garlic and ginger in 3 tablespoons hot oil. Remove from pan.
4. Carefully place the fried eggplants in the same pan and sauté for a few minutes.
5. Add Mixture A and cook until the sauce is well absorbed.

Tossed Bean Threads with Bean Sprouts

涼拌粉絲豆芽 (*Liang-pan-fên-ssu-tou-ya*)

See Page 48, 52

Quick and Easy Recipes

Continued from page 54

Tossed Bean Curd
    涼拌豆腐 (*Liang-pan-tou-fu*)

Sautéed Ground Meat with Peas
    炒 豌 豆 (*Ch'ao-wan-tou*)

Creamy Chinese Cabbage
    奶 油 白 菜 (*Nai-yu-pai-ts'ai*)

Chicken with Lemon Sauce
    西檸煎軟鶏 (*Hsi-ning-chien-juan-chi*)

Curried Shrimp
    咖喱 蝦 仁 (*Ka-li-hsia-jên*)

Tossed Bean Curd

涼拌豆腐
(*Liang-pan-tou-fu*)

Ingredients:
    1½ blocks of bean curd
    1 *p'i-tan*, shelled and cut into small bits
    2 tablespoons minced green onion or scallion
    few leaves of marsh parsley, or watercress

Mixture A
    1 teaspoon sugar
    1 teaspoon salt
    1 teaspoon sesame oil
    ¼ teaspoon *wu-hsiang-fên* (mixed Chinese spices)
    dash of monosodium glutamate

Instructions:
1. Boil bean curd briefly, cut into several pieces and drain well.
2. With wooden or rubber spatula, crush well-drained bean curd into small pieces in bowl.
3. Mix in prepared *p'i-tan* and green onion.
4. Add Mixture A and toss gently and thoroughly.
5. Remove to serving bowl and decorate with some green leaves like marsh parsley to add color.

Sautéed Ground Meat with Peas

炒 豌 豆
(*Ch'ao-wan-tou*)

Ingredients:

2½ cups peas, fresh or frozen
5½ oz. ground pork (or chicken)
1 tablespoon green onion, minced
1 teaspoon fresh ginger, minced
1 tablespoon wine
1 teaspoon cornstarch, dissolved in 2
　teaspoons water
cooking oil

Mixture A $\begin{cases} \text{2 tablespoons soy sauce} \\ \text{1 teaspoon sugar} \\ \frac{1}{8} \text{ teaspoon salt} \end{cases}$

Instructions:

1. Place peas in boiling salted water.
   Reduce heat and cook for 15 minutes.
   If frozen peas are used, just pour boiling water over them. Drain.
2. Sauté minced green onion and ginger
   in 1 tablespoon hot oil. Mix in ground
   meat and sprinkle with wine.
3. Add peas and Mixture A, stirring
   constantly. Thicken with dissolved
   cornstarch before removing to serving
   dish.

69

Creamy Chinese Cabbage

奶油白菜
(*Nai-yu-pai-ts'ai*)

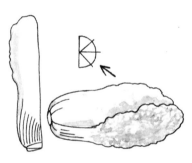

Ingredients:

½ Chinese cabbage, washed, cleaned, and cut length-wise into quarters, leaving core with leaves

6 cups soup stock

2 slices ham, shredded

1 tablespoon cornstarch, dissolved in 2 tablespoons water

cooking oil

Mixture A
- ½ cup milk
- ½ cup soup stock
- 1 tablespoon wine
- 1 tablespooon cooking oil
- 1 tablespoon juice from fresh ginger, grated and squeezed
- ½ teaspoon salt
- dash of monosodium glutamate

Instructions:

1. Sauté the quartered cabbage in 3 tablespoons hot oil. Add soup stock. Cover and simmer until tender.
2. Bring Mixture A to boil and quickly stir in dissolved cornstarch. When thickened remove from heat.
3. Arrange cooked cabbage carefully on serving plate, laying flat as in photo. Pour Mixture A over it and garnish with shredded ham.

Chicken with Lemon Sauce

西檸煎軟鷄
(*Hsi-ning-chien-juan-chi*)

Ingredients:

10 oz. boneless chicken, lightly pounded
with blunt edge of knife and cut into
bite-sized pieces
1 lemon
cooking oil
1 tablespoon cornstarch dissolved in 2
tablespoons water
minced parsley

Mixture A
- 1 tablespoon wine
- 1 tablespoon soy sauce
- 1 tablespoon cornstarch
- 1 egg white

Mixture B
- $\frac{1}{2}$ cup soup stock
- juice from $\frac{1}{2}$ lemon
- $1\frac{1}{2}$ tablespoons sugar
- $\frac{1}{2}$ tablespoon tomato catsup
- $\frac{1}{2}$ teaspoon salt
- dash of sesame oil, pepper

Instructions:

1. Dip chicken in Mixture A and deep-fry over medium heat. Drain.
2. Arrange on serving dish. Decorate with lemon thinly sliced into semi-circles.
3. Bring Mixture B to boil. Stir in dissolved cornstarch to thicken. Pour over the fried chicken and sprinkle with minced parsley.

Curried Shrimp

咖喱蝦仁
(*Ka-li-hsia-jên*)

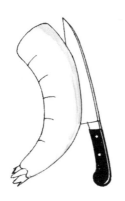

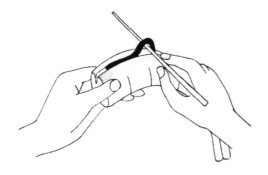

Ingredients:
1 1b. shelled shrimp
½ egg white
¼ teaspoon salt
1 teaspoon cornstarch
1 tablespoon wine
cooking oil

Mixture A {
2 tablespoons soup stock
1–2 teaspoons curry
    powder
½ teaspoon sugar
¼ teaspoon salt

Instructions:
1. Remove black vein of shelled shrimp and wash well in salt water. Drain.
2. Thoroughly mix together the egg white, salt, and cornstarch and dip shrimp into the mixture. Deep-fry over medium heat until almost done.
3. Heat 1 tablespoon cooking oil in pan. Add shrimp and sprinkle with wine. Add Mixture A, stirring quickly and thoroughly until done.

Recipes for Gourmets

Continued from page 56

Egg and Spinach Soup
    蛋花菠菜湯 (*Tan-hua-po-ts'ai-t'ang*)
Lemon Flavored Chicken
    檸 檬 鶏 (*Ning-mêng-chi*)
Chow-Mein
    炒 麵 (*Ch'ao-mien*)
Beef Steak Chinese Style
    中 式 牛 排 (*Chung-shih-niu-p'ai*)

Egg and Spinach Soup

蛋花菠菜湯
(*Tan-hua-po-ts'ai-t'ang*)

Ingredients:
¼ 1b. spinach leaves, washed and drained
6 cups soup stock
pinch of white pepper
2 eggs, lightly beaten

Instructions:
1. Bring soup stock to a boil. Season
   with white pepper. Add spinach leaves
   and pour beaten egg slowly into soup.
   Do not overcook.
2. Remove from heat immediately.

Lemon Flavored Chicken

檸 檬 鷄
(*Ning-mêng-chi*)

Ingredients:

2 1b. drumsticks; wash, drain, and wipe off

15 small onions, peeled

1 lemon; grate rind and squeeze out lemon juice

1 ginger, crushed

1 tablespoon wine

2 teaspoons cornstarch, dissolved in 4 teaspoons water

Mixture A
- $\frac{3}{4}$ cup chicken stock
- 1 tablespoon oyster sauce
- 2 tablespoons soy sauce
- 1 tablespoon sugar
- 1 teaspoon salt

Instructions:

1. Sauté crushed ginger in 3 tablespoons hot oil, add the chicken, and sprinkle with wine. Add onions and sauté a moment longer over high heat. Remove both chicken and onions to casserole, add Mixture A, cover and cook over high heat for 15 minutes.

2. Add lemon juice. Cook 5 minutes more. Just before removing from heat, sprinkle with lemon rind and thicken with dissolved cornstarch.

Chow-Mein

炒　麵
(*Ch'ao-mien*)

Ingredients:

3 packages Chinese noodles, boiled quickly, drained well, and sprinkled with sesame oil

4 oz. lean pork, shredded

½ egg white

1 teaspoon cornstarch

4–5 dried Chinese mushrooms, soaked, stems removed, and shredded

5 cups bean sprouts, washed and drained

4 leeks, washed and cut into 2-inch lengths

1 tablespoon wine

1 teaspoon cornstarch, dissolved in 2 teaspoons water

cooking oil

Mixture A
- 1 tablespoon oyster sauce
- 1 tablespoon soy sauce
- ½ cup soup stock
- ¼ teaspoon salt
- ¼ teaspoon sugar
- dash of sesame oil, pepper, and monosodium glutamate

Instructions:

1. Dip shredded pork into mixture of egg white and cornstarch and fry slowly over low heat until color turns pale. Drain.

2. Sauté bean sprouts, leeks, mushrooms and pork in 3 tablespoons hot oil. Sprinkle with wine. Add Mixture A and bring to boil. Thicken with dissolved cornstarch.

3. Heat 4–5 tablespoons cooking oil in a big pan and sauté noodles over high heat turning thoroughly. Remove to platter and pour the thickened mixture over it. Serve warm.

75

Beef Steak Chinese Style

中 式 牛 排

(*Chung-shih-niu-p'ai*)

Ingredients:

1 1b. fillet of beef, sliced ½-inch thick and sprinkled lightly with salt and pepper.
3 tomatoes, sliced
⅔ 1b. string beans, washed and cut in 2-inch lengths
1 egg white
1 tablespoon cornstarch
1 teaspoon cornstarch, dissolved in 2 teaspoons water
cooking oil

Mixture A
{
1 tablespoon wine
2 tablespoons soy sauce
2 tablespoons cooking oil
½ teaspoon sugar
}

Mixture B
{
1 tablespoon cooking oil
3 tablespoons catsup
3 tablespoons Worcestershire sauce
1 tablespoon vinegar
1 teaspoon sugar
}

Instructions:

1. Marinate beef slices in Mixture A for 30 minutes.
2. While marinating beef, sauté prepared string beans in 2 tablespoons hot oil. Add 1 teaspoon salt and 1 cup water. Cover and simmer until tender. Drain.
3. Blend 1 tablespoon cornstarch and 1 egg white; dip beef slices into this mixture. Fry meat slowly in deep oil. Drain.
4. Heat Mixture B in pan. Mix in fried beef and cook briefly over high heat. Thicken with dissolved cornstarch. Remove to platter. Arrange tomato slices and cooked beans around beef.

76

How to make chicken soup stock

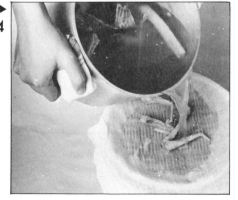

I. Using whole chicken with bones
* 1 whole chicken, thoroughly washed
* $\frac{1}{2}$ green onion, lightly struck with dull edge of knife
* 2-inch piece ginger, lightly struck with dull edge of knife
* 1 tablespoon wine

1. Place chicken in boiling water, then remove from pan. **(1)**
2. Pour 12 cups water in heavy kettle and put in chicken, green onion and ginger. Add wine and cook over high heat until stock starts to boil. **(2)**
3. Reduce heat and cook uncovered gently for more than an hour, removing scum occasionally. **(3)**
4. Take out chicken and immediately strain the stock. **(4)**

II. Using wing tips (or bony parts)
* about $1\frac{1}{2}$ lb. wing tips (or necks, backs)
* 12 cups water
* 1 bouillon cube
* $\frac{1}{2}$ green onion, lightly struck with dull edge of knife
* 2 slices fresh ginger, lightly struck with dull edge of knife
* 1 tablespoon wine

Method is the same as for whole chicken. When you wish to preserve stock for 3–4 days, store in covered jars and freeze. During hot seasons, it should be taken out of refrigerator and boiled once a day.

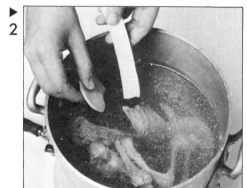

Hors d'Oeuvres

Continued from page 58

Sweet-Sour Chinese Cabbage ①
辣 白 菜 (*La-pai-ts'ai*)

Sautéed Chinese Mushrooms ②
滷 冬 菇 (*Lu-tung-ku*)

Savory Prawns ③
油 爆 蝦 (*Yu-pao-hsia*)

Steamed Chicken ④
白 切 鷄 (*Pai-ch'ieh-chi*)

Molded *P'i-tan* Eggs ⑤
皮蛋鮮蛋糕 (*P'i-tan-hsien-tan-kao*)

Vinegared Jellyfish with Cucumber ⑥
拌 海 蜇 皮 (*Pan-hai-chê-p'i*)

Fried Honey Walnuts
蜜汁胡桃 (*Mi-chih-hu-t'ao*)

Tossed Celery Shanghai Style
拌 芹 菜 (*Pan-ch'in-ts'ai*)

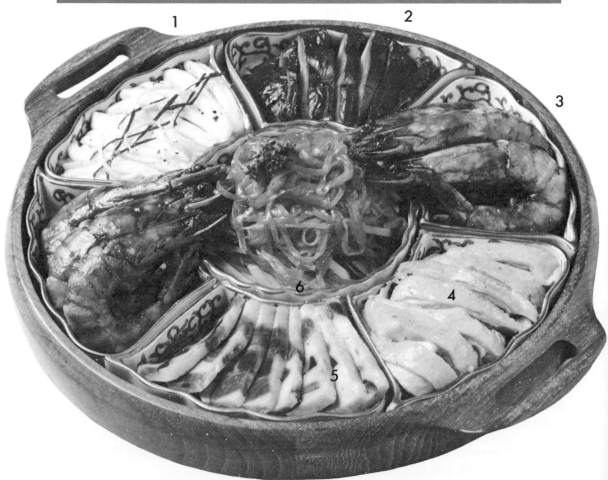

Sweet-Sour Chinese Cabbage

辣 白 菜
(*La-pai-ts'ai*)

Ingredients:
- ½ Chinese cabbage
- 2 dried hot red peppers, seeded and shredded lengthwise
- 1 1-inch fresh ginger, thinly sliced then shredded
- 1 tablespoon *hua-chiao* (Chinese pepper) seeds
- 1 tablespoon sesame oil

Mixture A
- ½ cup vinegar
- ½ cup sugar
- 1 tablespoon soy sauce
- 1 tablespoon salt
- dash of monosodium glutamate

Instructions:
1. Cut cabbage into 2-inch widths. The white part around the core should be sliced into ½-inch pieces.
2. Mix together the cabbage, shredded ginger and hot red pepper and pour Mixture A over it.
3. Parch *hua-chiao* and grind in mortar, then fry quickly in sesame oil. Mix into (2). Let stand 4 hours, stirring occasionally.

Note: *If Chinese cabbage is not obtainable, ordinary cabbage can be used instead.*

Sautéed Chinese Mushrooms

滷 冬 菇
(*Lu-tung-ku*)

Ingredients:
- 5 large dried Chinese mushrooms
- cooking oil
- dash of sesame oil

Mixture A
- ⅓ cup soup stock
- 2 tablespoons soy sauce
- 2 tablespoons sugar
- 1 tablespoon wine
- ⅛ teaspoon salt
- dash of monosodium glutamate

Instructions:

1. Soak dried mushrooms in lukewarm water until tender. Remove stems and squeeze out water. Sauté in 1 tablespoon hot oil. Reduce heat. Add A sauce and cook slowly until very little liquid is left in pan. Sprinkle with a few drops of sesame oil for glaze and flavor. Cool.
2. Slice lengthwise into thin strips and arrange on serving dish.

Savory Prawns

油 爆 蝦
(*Yu-pao-hsia*)

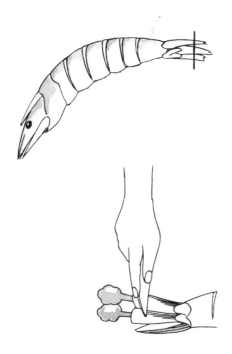

Ingredients:

6 prawns
1 tablespoon wine
cooking oil
dash of sesame oil

Mixture A
{
1½ tablespoons soy sauce
1½ tablespoons sugar
1 tablespoon wine
1 teaspoon vinegar
1 tablespoon fresh ginger juice
}

Instructions:

1. Cut off hairy little "legs" on the sides of the prawn shells and a little bit from the tip of the tails. Squeeze out water from tails, remove black veins, wash, drain, then sprinkle with wine. Deep-fry quickly over medium heat. Drain.
2. Sauté Mixture A in 3 tablespoons hot oil and add the prawns. Keep stirring over high heat until almost no liquid is left in pan. Just before removing from heat, sprinkle with sesame oil for glaze.

Steamed Chicken

白 切 鶏 (*Pai-ch'ieh-chi*)

See page 38

Molded *P'i-tan* Eggs

皮蛋鮮蛋糕
(*P'i-tan-hsien-tan-kao*)

Ingredients:

3 *p'i-tan* egg yolks
5 eggs
cooking oil

Mixture A
- ½ cup soup stock
- ½ teaspoon salt
- ½ teaspoon sugar
- dash of monosodium glutamate

Instructions:

1. Cut *p'i-tan* egg yolks in ½-inch cubes.
2. Stir eggs lightly just till whites and yolks are mixed. Add Mixture A and pour into flat container greased with oil. Mix in cubes of *p'i-tan* yolk.
3. Steam over low heat for 20 minutes. When center part is set, remove from heat. When almost cool, take out of the container. Slice thinly and arrange on serving dish.

Vinegared Jellyfish with Cucumber

拌 海 蜇 皮
(*Pan-hai-chê-p'i*)

Ingredients:

⅔ 1b. dried salted jellyfish, either in 1 piece or shredded
1 cucumber, julienned

Mixture A
- 4 tablespoons vinegar
- 2 tablespoons soy sauce
- 2 tablespoons sugar
- 1 teaspoon salt
- dash of monosodium glutamate, sesame oil and pepper

Instructions:

1. Soak jellyfish in water overnight. Wash thoroughly and cut into 4-inch strings. Place in bowl and pour very hot water over them. When shrunk, remove to cold water and drain.
2. Combine jellyfish with Mixture A. Let stand 15 minutes.
3. Arrange cucumber on serving dish, then place jellyfish on top.

Note: *Soaking in water overnight gives the best results even when shredded jellyfish is used.*

Fried Honey Walnuts

蜜汁胡桃
(*Mi-chih-hu-t'ao*)

Ingredients:

5½ oz. shelled walnuts
honey
sugar
cooking oil

Instructions:

1. Dip shelled walnuts in honey and let stand for 3 nights. Drain. Coat walnuts with sugar.
2. Fry over medium heat until golden brown. Cool before arranging in dish.

Tossed Celery, Shanghai Style

拌 芹 菜
(*Pan-ch'in-ts'ai*)

Ingredients:

¾ lb. celery, cleaned and cut into sticks about 1½-inches long

Mixture A
- 3 tablespoons vinegar
- 1 tablespoon soy sauce
- 1 tablespoon sesame oil
- 2 tablespoons sugar
- 2 teaspoons *tou-pan-chiang* (Chinese hot sauce)
- ¼ teaspoon salt
- dash of monosodium glutamate

Instructions:

1. Place prepared celery in a bowl. Add Mixture A. Gently toss celery sticks and let stand for 15 minutes.
2. Drain well and arrange in dish.

82

(*Continued from page 13*)
Deep-Fried Chicken

炸 子 鶏
(*Cha-tzu-chi*)

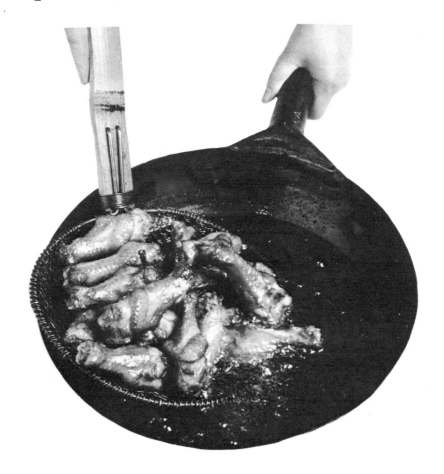

Ingredients:

2 lb. chicken legs with thigh cut into 2
  pieces and drumstick left whole
cooking oil
dash of *hua-chiao-yen* (Chinese pepper
  powder mixed with salt)
oil for frying
lemon

Mixture A $\begin{cases} 3 \text{ tablespoons soy sauce} \\ 1 \text{ tablespoon wine} \end{cases}$

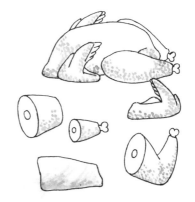

Instructions:

1. Marinate chicken in Mixture A for 30
   minutes. Drain and wipe off lightly.
2. Fry in deep oil until golden brown.
   Drain.
3. Serve hot with *hua-chiao-yen* and
   lemon wedges.

(*Continued from page 33*)
Fried Egg, Shanghai Style

芙蓉炒蟹粉
(*Fu-jung-ch'ao-hsieh-fên*)

Ingredients:

'2 oz. bean threads cut into 4-inch lengths
3 egg whites, beaten until fluffy   **(2)**
5 oz. boiled bamboo shoots, diced
1 can (7 oz.) crab meat, boned, flaked, drained, and sprinkled with 1 tablespoon wine
cooking oil

Mixture A
{
$\frac{1}{4}$ cup soup stock
$\frac{1}{2}$ teaspoon salt
few drops of sesame oil
dash of pepper
dash of monosodium glutamate
}

Instructions:

1. Heat the oil in pan, and deep-fry bean threads about 3 minutes or until crispy.   **(1)**
2. Combine beaten egg whites, crab meat, bamboo shoots and Mixture A.   **(3)**
3. Heat pan and pour in 2 tablespoons cooking oil. Continue heating until bottom and sides of pan are thoroughly greased and hot.
4. Gently pour egg mixture into pan over high heat. When center part is half set, turn over and fry the other side. Repeat 3–4 times.   **(4)**
5. Arrange fried bean threads and place fried egg on top. Serve immediately.

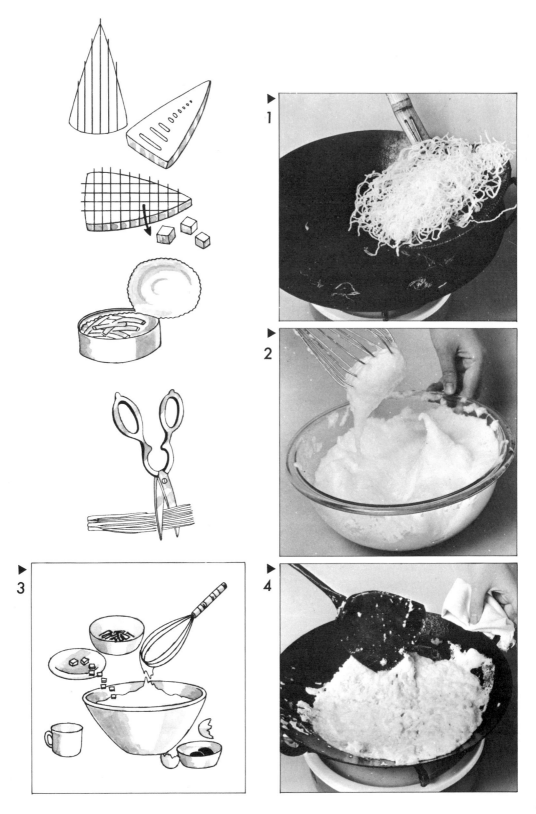

(Continued from page 1)

Broccoli with Prawns

西蘭花蝦球
(*Hsi-lan-hua-hsia-ch'iu*)

Ingredients:

10 prawns, cleaned, shelled except tails
10 oz. broccoli, cleaned, leaves and tough parts removed
3 slices fresh ginger root
1 clove garlic, minced
1 tablespoon wine
cooking oil

Mixture A
- 1 tablespoon soup stock
- 1 tablespoon oyster sauce
- 1 teaspoon salt
- $\frac{1}{4}$ teaspoon sugar
- dash of sesame oil, pepper, monosodium glutamate

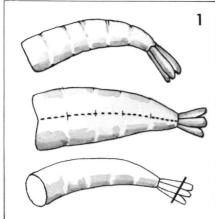

Instructions:

1. Remove black veins of cleaned, shelled prawns. Slice in half, along back without cutting through. Wipe off. **(1)**
2. Cook broccoli in boiling salt water over medium heat for 7–8 minutes. Remove to cold water. Drain well. **(2)**
3. Stir-fry prepared prawns in deep fat and set aside. **(3)**
4. Sauté minced garlic and ginger slices in 3 tablespoons oil. Add broccoli and prawns and sprinkle with wine. Stir in quickly Mixture A over high heat.
5. Place broccoli on serving dish and surround with prawns, or put prawns in center and surround with broccoli.

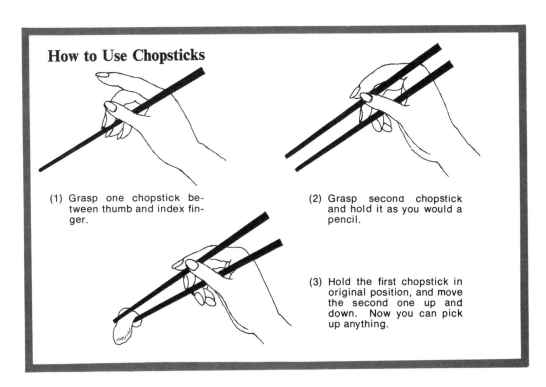

How to Use Chopsticks

(1) Grasp one chopstick between thumb and index finger.

(2) Grasp second chopstick and hold it as you would a pencil.

(3) Hold the first chopstick in original position, and move the second one up and down. Now you can pick up anything.

How to make *Chiao-tzu* wrapping

1. Add $1\frac{1}{2}$ cups water to $3\frac{1}{2}$ cups sifted
    pastry flour and blend well by hand
    until soft as ear-lobe. Wrap with damp
    cloth and let stand 2 hours.   **(1–3)**
2. Pat gently on sides of the cloth with
    water to unwrap easily. Place on
    board dusted with flour and shape
    into a roll 1-inch in diameter. Cut into
    $\frac{3}{4}$-inch lengths, and roll out each
    piece into thin circles.   **(4–6)**

1

2

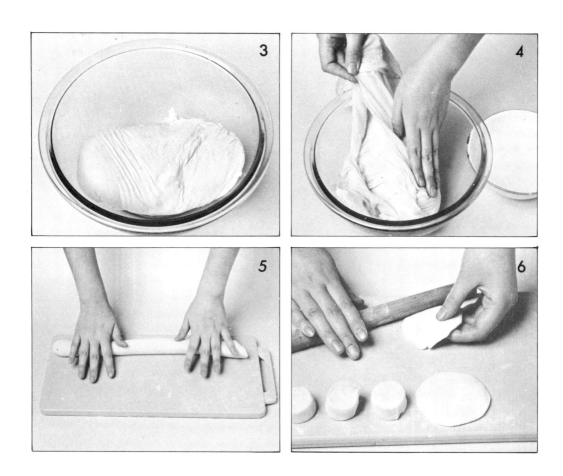

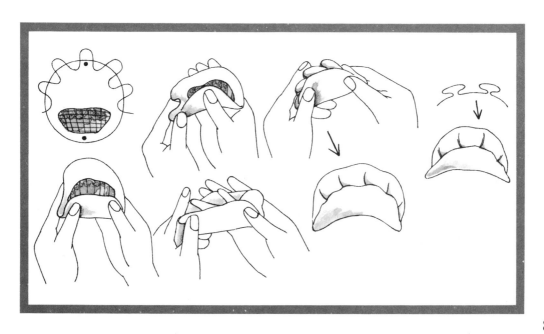

How to make Spring roll (or Egg-roll) wrappers

To make spring roll skin:

1. Sift 3½ cups flour into a large bowl.
2. Pour in 1½ cups warm water, and knead well.
3. Cover with moistened cloth and let stand for 2 hours.
4. Dust flour on a board. Roll the dough and make a stick. Cut into 1-inch lengths.
5. Roll out the dough, and press each into rounds about 2½ inches in diameter.

To stuff spring roll:

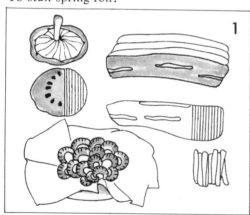

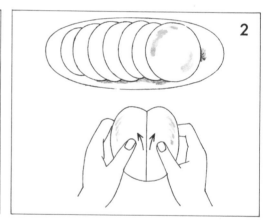

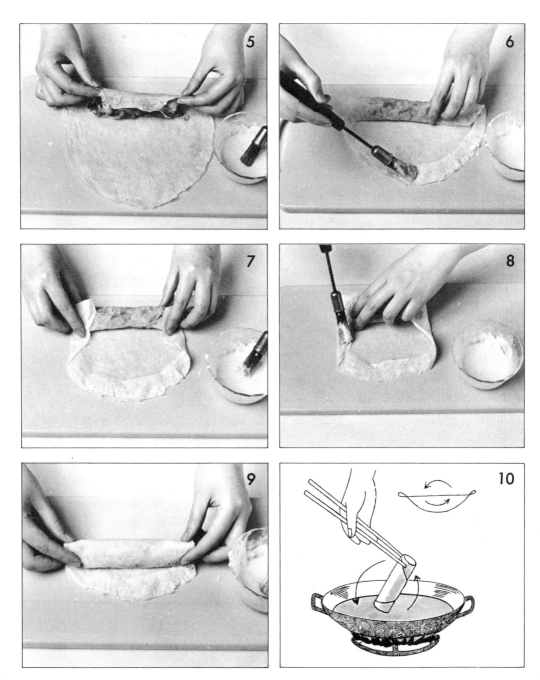

How to prepare dried noodles

1. Bring plenty of water to boil in a large pot. Add 4 bundles of dried noodles. **(1–3)**
2. Bring to boil again and add 1 cup water. Add water twice. **(4)**
3. Squeeze out water and drain. Mix with a few drops of sesame oil immediately. **(5–6)**

Seasoning and Spices

Brown Bean Sauce: 豆辨醬 (*tou-pan-chiang*)
Made from broad beans and red pepper. Very hot to taste.

Cinnamon: 桂 皮 (*kuei-p'i*)
Whole or ground: used in braising, simmering, and for pudding.

Cloves: 丁 香 (*ting-hsiang*)
Dried .... whole for pork and stew
Ground .... for baked dishes

Coriander seeds: 芫荽米 (*yuan-sui-mi*)

Dried Ginger Root: 三 肉 (*san-jou*)

Fennel Seeds: 小 茴 (*hsiao-hui*)

Five Spice Powder: 五香粉 (*wu-hsiang-fên*)
Compound of ground Szechwan pepper, cloves, cinnamon, fennel seeds and star anise.

Hoisin Sauce: 海鮮醬 (*hai-hsien-chiang*)
Brown-red sweet bean-paste sauce. Used as a table condiment. Canned.

Hot Sauce: 辣 油 (*la-yu*)
Sesame oil with chili peppers.

Kan-ts'ao: 甘 草 (*kan-ts'ao*) Liquorice

Orange Peel: 陳 皮 (*ch'ên-p'i*)
Dried orange peel. Used to season stewed dishes. Before using, soak in water until soft. Squeeze out water and mince.

Oyster Sauce: 蠔 油 (*hao-yu*)
Fresh oyster preserved in salt, fermented and skimmed. Used to season beef and vegetable dishes.

Rice Vinegar: 醋 (*ts'u*)

Salted and Fermented Black Beans: 豆 豉 (*tou-chih*)
Used to darken sauce for stewed fish and meat dishes.

Sesame Oil: 麻 油 (*ma-yu*)
Potent oil of sesame seeds.

Shrimp Paste: 蝦 醬 (*hsia-chiang*)
Thick paste (purple-white) made from shellfish. Used as a flavoring agent.

Soy Sauce: 醬 油 (*chiang-yu*)
Salty, brown, soybean extract, made from fermented soy beans, wheat, yeast and salt. Available in two shades, dark or light.

Star Anise: 八 角 , 大 茴 (*pa-chiao , ta-hui*)
Looks like a star-shaped seed. Is used whole in stewed dishes.

Szechwan Pepper: 花 椒 (*hua-chiao*)
A tangy Chinese spice, available ground or in seeds.
花椒塩 (*hua-chiao-yen*):
Mix toasted and ground seeds with salt, for a tastier deep-fried dish.

Ts'ao-kuo: 草 果 (*ts'ao-kuo*)
Whole or ground: used in braising or simmering.

Ingredients

Agar-agar: 東洋菜 (*tung-yang-ts'ai*)
Dried stick made from seaweed.

Bamboo Shoots: 竹 筍 (*chu-sun*)
Canned or fresh young shoots.

Bean Curd Cake: 豆 腐 (*tou-fu*)
Bean cake (white and soft square cake).

Bean Sprouts: 豆 芽 (*tou-ya*)
Vegetable; mung bean sprouts; fresh or canned.

Bean Threads: 粉 絲 (*fên-su*)
Fine transparent noodles made from green beans.

Celery Cabbage: 紹 菜 (*shao-ts'ai*)
Savory cabbage.

Chinese Cabbage (White): 白菜 (*pai-t'sai*):
Bok Choy Vegetable; white stalks with large green leaves outside.

Chinese Chives: 韭 菜 (*chiu-ts'ai*)

Chinese Parsley: 香 菜 (*hsiang-ts'ai*)
Coriander herb, looks like parsley. Dried coriander seeds are called 芫荽米 (*yuan-sui-mi*).

Cloud Ears: 木 耳 (*mu-êrh*)
A cup-shaped mushroom with spongy texture.

Dried Shrimp: 蝦 米 (*Hsia-mi*)
Tiny shelled and dried shrimps.

Dried Scallop: 干 貝 (*kan-pei*)
Shellfish.

Fresh Garlic: 大 蒜 (*ta-suan*)

Jellyfish: 海蜇皮 (*hai-chê-p'i*)
Dried seafood.

Giant White Radish: 大頭菜 (*ta-tou-t'sai*)
White root vegetable.

Mustard Greens: 芥 菜 (*chieh-ts'ai*)
Green vegetable with leafy stalk.

Noodles: 麵 (*mien*)
Fine noodles made from flour.

Preserved Egg: 皮 蛋 (*p'i-tan*)
Duck egg aged and preserved in paste of ashes, lime tea, and salt for several months.

Rice Stick: 米 粉 (*mi-fên*)
Thin stick similar to vermicelli.

Snow Peas: 豌 莢 (*wan-chia*)
Edible pod peas.

Water Chestnuts: 馬 蹄 (*ma-t'i*)

Winter Mushroom and Flower Mushroom: 冬 菇 , 花 菇 (*tung-ku, hua-ku*)

Index

MEMO